WILDWORLD

Alligators & Crocodiles

Karen Dudley

A & C Black · London

This edition published 1999 in Great Britain by
A & C Black (Publishers) Ltd, 35 Bedford Row, London WC1R 4JH
First published 1997 in Canada by Weigl Educational Publishers Limited.

ISBN 0-7136-5134-2
A Cataloguing in Publication Data (CIP) record of this book is available from the British Library.

Printed and bound in Canada

Project Editor
Lauri Seidlitz

Design and Illustration
Warren Clark

Editor
Kathy DeVico

Copy Editors
Janice Parker, Leslie Strudwick

Layout
Chris Bowerman

Consultants
J. Whitfield Gibbons is Professor of Ecology at the University of Georgia's Savannah River Ecology Laboratory.

Dr Frank Mazzotti is a wildlife scientist at the University of Florida. He is also a member of the IUCN Crocodile Specialist Group.

Acknowledgments
The publisher wishes to thank Warren Rylands for inspiring this series.

Photograph Credits

American Museum of Natural History: page 54 (Courtesy Department of Library Services, Neg. No. 46808, Photo. Julian A. Dimock, Feb. 24, 1906); **Corel Corporation**: cover, pages 8, 11, 13, 14, 19, 21, 31, 32, 42, 44, 45, 59, 60, 61; **Florida Game and Fresh Water Fish Commission**: page 56; **Photofest**: page 46; **Wilf Schurig**: pages 4, 23, 43; **Tom Stack and Associates**: pages 12 (Joe McDonald), 20 (David M. Dennis), 26 (Nancy Adams); **Dave Taylor**: pages 10, 15, 16, 17, 18, 24, 29, 30, 35, 38, 40, 41; **U.S. Fish and Wildlife Service**: page 36 (Tom Worthington); **Visuals Unlimited**: pages 22 (Dale Jackson), 25 (Kirtley-Perkins), 27, 39 (Rick Poley), 34 (Fritz Pölking); **E. Melanie Watt**: page 28; **John C. Whyte**: page 6.

Every reasonable effort has been made to trace ownership and to obtain permission to reprint copyright material. The publishers would be pleased to have any errors or omissions brought to their attention so that they may be corrected in subsequent printings.

Contents

Introduction

Crocodilians date back to the time of the dinosaurs.

Opposite: A crocodilian has eyes on the top of its head so it can see above water while its body is submerged.

Alligators and crocodiles are reptiles. Reptiles are a class of animals that includes snakes, lizards, turtles, and a species called the tuatara. Alligators and crocodiles are part of a reptilian order called **crocodilians**. This group also includes gharials and a group of reptiles closely related to alligators, the caymans. Crocodilians date back to the time of the dinosaurs. They are one of the oldest and largest groups of living reptiles.

Read on, and learn the differences between alligators, crocodiles, and gharials. Find out why crocodilians are good parents. Discover how alligators can survive in temperatures well below freezing. You will learn what crocodilians eat and how they hunt. You will also find out why they sometimes spin in a "death roll".

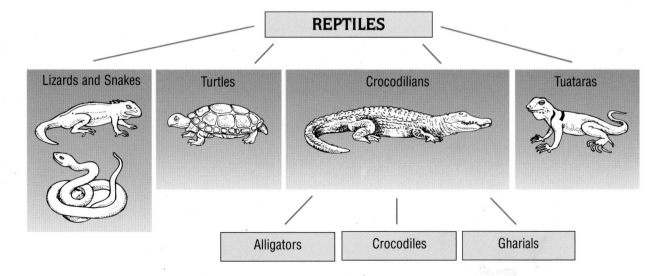

REPTILES

Lizards and Snakes · Turtles · Crocodilians · Tuataras

Alligators · Crocodiles · Gharials

Features

The differences between alligators and crocodiles can be found by looking at their heads and teeth.

Opposite: Aside from differences in its teeth and snout, this cayman shares many features with its scaly cousins, the crocodiles and gharials.

A ll crocodilian species share certain features, including body shape and senses. What makes each species different? The answer can be found by looking at their heads and teeth.

Alligators and caymans belong to the same family within the crocodilian order. They have shorter, wider snouts than crocodiles and gharials. When an alligator or cayman closes its mouth, its fourth lower tooth is usually hidden by its upper jaw. Some cayman species have bony ridges, called spectacles, between their eyes. Alligators do not have spectacles.

Crocodiles have slender, pointy snouts and relatively flat foreheads. When a crocodile closes its mouth, its lower fourth tooth is still visible.

Gharials are easy to tell apart from the other crocodilians. Their foreheads are high, and their snouts are very slender with many small, sharp teeth.

CROCODILIAN HEAD SHAPES

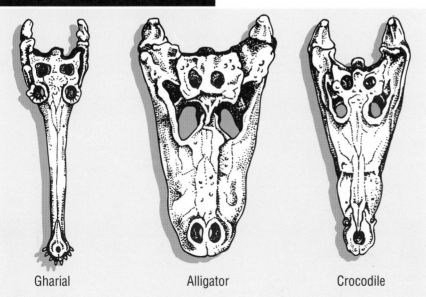

Gharial   Alligator   Crocodile

Living Fossils

The crocodilian family tree goes back a long way. The crocodilians' original ancestor lived during the Mesozoic Era, which began 225 million years ago and ended 65 million years ago. This era is also known as the Age of the Reptiles, because dinosaurs lived during this time.

Crocodilians evolved from a group of animals known as **thecodonts**. Other animals, like dinosaurs and modern birds, also evolved from thecodonts. This means that crocodilians are very distantly related to birds. In fact, some scientists believe that crocodilians are more closely related to birds than to any other living creature.

About 65 million years ago, the dinosaurs died out. Scientists are not sure why dinosaurs became extinct. Some believe a huge meteorite hit Earth at this time, causing severe changes in the weather. Many animals became extinct at this time.

The ancestors of this Galápagos giant tortoise and crocodilians lived with the dinosaurs.

Along with leatherback turtles and Galápagos tortoises, crocodilians were among the only large reptiles to survive. Crocodilians are sometimes called living fossils because they look very similar to their 65-million-year-old ancestors.

LIFE SPAN

Biologists do not know how long wild crocodilians live. The oldest documented American alligator in captivity lived to be 66 years old. Most scientists believe that wild crocodilians probably do not live this long. Missing teeth and other signs of aging have been found in captive crocodilians that were over 50 years old. From this, biologists estimate that 50 years is most likely the maximum life span of a wild crocodilian.

Size

Crocodilians can vary greatly in size, depending on the species. In general, females are smaller than males. Some alligator species grow at different rates in different parts of their range. Many scientists think crocodilians continue to grow throughout their lifetime, while others believe crocodilians may stop growing when they reach maturity. The growth rate is fastest during the first two years of life. After this, the crocodilian's growth slows down.

CROCODILIAN SIZES

Species	Latin Name	Maximum adult male size
American alligator	*Alligator mississippiensis*	4.5 metres
American crocodile	*Crocodylus acutus*	6 metres
Australian freshwater crocodile	*Crocodylus johnsoni*	3 metres
Black cayman	*Melanosuchus niger*	4.5 to 6 metres
Broad-snouted cayman	*Cayman latirostris*	2 to 3.5 metres
Chinese alligator	*Alligator sinensis*	2 metres
Common cayman	*Cayman crocodilus*	2.8 metres
Cuban crocodile	*Crocodylus rhombifer*	3.5 to 4.9 metres
Dwarf cayman	*Paleosuchus palpebrosus*	1.6 metres
Dwarf crocodile	*Osteolaemus tetraspis*	2 metres
Gharial	*Gavialis gangeticus*	6 to 7 metres
Morelet's crocodile	*Crocodylus moreletti*	3 metres
Mugger crocodile	*Crocodylus palustris*	4.5 metres
New Guinea crocodile	*Crocodylus novaeguineae*	3.5 metres
Nile crocodile	*Crocodylus niloticus*	5.5 metres
Orinoco crocodile	*Crocodylus intermedius*	6 metres
Philippine crocodile	*Crocodylus mindorensis*	3 metres
Saltwater crocodile	*Crocodylus porosus*	7 metres
Siamese crocodile	*Crocodylus siamensis*	3 to 4 metres
Slender-snouted crocodile	*Crocodylus cataphractus*	3 to 4 metres
Smooth-fronted cayman	*Paleosuchus trigonatus*	2.3 metres
Tomistoma	*Tomistoma schlegelii*	5 metres
Yacare cayman	*Cayman yacare*	2.8 metres

Scales, Scutes, and Skin

Crocodilian skin has two layers. The outer layer is a hard, hornlike material called **keratin**. The keratin thickens to form sections called **scales** that lie flat against the crocodilian's body. These scales differ in size, shape, and strength, depending on where they are located on the crocodilian's body.

Unlike fish scales, which are separate from one another, a crocodilian's scales are connected. Scales do not grow in size. As an animal grows, it must shed its scales. When snakes grow, they lose their entire body casing in large patches. When crocodilians grow, they lose individual scales separately. This difference is because snake scales overlap, causing the skin to fall off in pieces. Crocodilian scales are connected by thinner areas of tissue that break as the animal grows.

The inner layer of a crocodilian's skin lies beneath the scales. It is made up of tissues and small bony plates known as **osteoderms**. These osteoderms are a crocodilian's armour. They strengthen the scales and help protect the reptile from injury.

A crocodilian's skin varies in colour, depending on the species. Along their backs, crocodilians may be black, reddish-brown, or olive green. In general, a crocodilian's stomach is lighter in colour, ranging from off-white to light brown. Many species also have bands or spots of darker colour along their tails and backs. In some species, a juvenile's skin is quite different in colour and pattern to an adult's skin.

*Some species of crocodilians have large scales that stick up from their backs and tails. These raised scales are known as **scutes**.*

Blood and Body Temperature

Reptiles are called cold-blooded, but this does not mean that their blood is cold. In fact, a crocodilian that is basking in the sun may have a body temperature of 35°C. Normal human body temperature is 37°C. What cold-blooded really means is that the animal's body temperature rises and falls, depending on the temperature of its environment. Unlike mammals, crocodilians and other reptiles cannot shiver when they are cold. They do not have feathers or fur to keep themselves warm. Instead, they must control their body temperature through their behaviour.

In hot climates, crocodilians keep their blood cool by staying underwater for much of the day and going up onto land for the night. In cool climates, alligators and crocodiles bask in the sun to warm their blood. At night, they retreat to ponds or lakes where the water stays warmer than the air.

During the day, you might see a crocodilian basking in the sun with its mouth wide open. This is not a sign of hunger. The skin inside a crocodilian's mouth is thin, with many blood vessels near the surface. By lying with its mouth open, the reptile can cool itself down and prevent overheating. In a similar way, a swimming crocodilian may cool itself by opening its mouth. This allows the water inside its mouth to evaporate.

This Nile crocodile opens its mouth to keep cool while in the hot sun.

Special Adaptations

Crocodilians have several features that help make them excellent predators.

Sight

Crocodilians have good eyesight and they can see in colour. Their eyes have slitlike pupils. This is because they are **nocturnal**, or night-time, hunters. In the dark, a slitlike pupil can open wider than a round pupil. This means that more light can enter the eye, allowing the crocodilian to see better.

Crocodilians also have a special feature that helps them hunt underwater. They have eyelids like humans, but they also have a third, clear eyelid. This third eyelid protects the eye and allows the reptile to see underwater. Although crocodilians have some underwater vision, they must rely on other senses to hunt because the water is often too murky for them to see well.

In bright sunlight, the pupil of a crocodilian's eye becomes narrow and vertical to reduce the light entering its eye.

Hearing

Crocodilians have an excellent sense of hearing. They can even hear their unhatched young calling from inside their eggs. Crocodilian ears are protected by a movable flap. When a crocodilian dives, it covers its ears with the flap, preventing water from entering its ear canal.

Smell

A crocodilian's nostrils are located on top of its snout. This allows the reptile to breathe, even when its body is completely underwater. When the crocodilian dives, it pinches its nostrils together so water does not get into its nose. Crocodilians have a very good sense of smell. Much of their brain is used for this sense. Experiments have shown that even young crocodilians respond to smells in the air.

Jaws and Teeth

Crocodilians can snap their jaws shut with amazing force. The jaws of a large adult crocodilian can exert a crushing force equal to 10,821 kilograms. This is strong enough to pierce a turtle's shell or crush a cow's leg. Although these jaw-closing muscles are very strong, the muscles that open the jaw are quite weak. The mouth of a 2-metre-long crocodilian can be kept closed with a single elastic band.

A crocodilian has about 28 to 32 teeth in its lower jaw, and 30 to 40 teeth in its upper jaw. The teeth are sharp and have cutting edges. They are ideal for grabbing and tearing, but they cannot be used for chewing. Instead, a crocodilian tears its prey apart before swallowing it in pieces.

As the teeth break or wear down, they are replaced. New teeth grow in under the existing old teeth. This occurs in waves. In young crocodilians, the back teeth are replaced first. In adults the reverse is true. Only every second tooth is replaced at a time. In this way, crocodilians still have enough teeth to hunt even when new ones are growing in. Tooth replacement continues throughout a crocodilian's lifetime, slowing down as the reptile ages. A Nile crocodile that has grown to 3.9 metres in length may have had 45 sets of teeth! Very old crocodilians may lose teeth permanently.

Crocodilian teeth are shaped like cones.

Locomotion on Land

Crocodilians do not move as well on land as they do in water. They usually avoid travelling very far on land. They do, however, leave the water to build nests and lay eggs, seek shelter from heat and cold, or escape from a threat. If their habitat dries up, the reptiles may have to go on a longer journey to find a new watery home.

Crocodilians are **quadrupeds**, which means they walk on all four legs. There are three main kinds of land locomotion: the high walk, the belly crawl, and the gallop.

When using the high walk, a crocodilian's hind legs are held almost beneath its body. In this way, its belly and tail are kept high off the ground. This walk is similar to the motion of a mammal's walk. Crocodilians reach speeds of .3 to .5 kilometres per hour. Sometimes they can speed up a bit, but they must be careful. If a crocodilian moves too fast in a high walk, it can lose its balance and fall.

The belly crawl movement is similar to the way a lizard walks. The crocodilian holds its belly close to the ground, with its legs stretched out to the side. Twisting its body from side to side, the crocodilian pulls itself along with its legs and slithers across the ground. This type of locomotion is often used when a crocodilian is startled or wants to slip back into the water quietly.

Most crocodilians are also capable of a gallop. Using its hind legs to push, the crocodilian bounds forward in a kind of jump. It holds its tail up from the ground. When using the gallop, a crocodilian can reach speeds of about 18 kilometres per hour. Most crocodilians have trouble moving quickly on land for more than a few metres.

Unlike other reptiles, crocodilians have a special ankle joint that allows their feet to twist and turn so that walking on land is easier.

Locomotion in Water

Crocodilians are skilled and graceful swimmers. Some species, like gharials, rarely go up onto land at all except to build nests and lay eggs. When moving through its watery habitat, a crocodilian holds its legs close to its body. It propels itself through the water like a torpedo, sweeping its long, powerful tail back and forth. If the reptile is chasing prey or being hunted

itself, it can also jump out of the water in a kind of "tail walk" similar to that of a dolphin.

Crocodilians also spend time floating just beneath the surface of the water. Their legs are held out to the side to help them float more easily. Sometimes when a crocodilian is floating, it may hold its body almost vertically in the water. As long as its nostrils are close to the surface, the reptile can relax and let the water support its body.

Crocodilians can remain almost vertical in the water for long periods of time. Crocodilians can also move vertically on land, but they can do it for only a few seconds, as they jump or lunge at prey.

Crocodilian Society

Crocodilians have an active social life that includes many ways of communicating with other crocodilians.

Opposite: A lone American alligator is a rare sight in the forest.

Before the 1970s, little was known about crocodilian society. It is difficult to study the behaviour of animals that spend most of their time in the water. There had been a few attempts to study American alligators and Nile crocodiles, but most other species had been ignored. In the last two decades, people have become more aware of the importance of conserving endangered species. This awareness led to studies of more species of crocodilians. What the scientists discovered surprised many people.

Most people think of crocodilians as solitary predators that spend their time lying in the water, waiting for unsuspecting prey. Although crocodilians are inactive for much of the time, and do lie in ambush when they hunt, they are not solitary creatures. In fact, crocodilians have an active social life that includes many ways of communicating with other crocodilians.

A group of Cuban crocodiles by the shore is a more common sight.

Nursery Groups

Crocodilian social groups form at birth. Young crocodilians, or **hatchlings**, often stay near the nest after they have hatched. They form groups known as nursery groups or **pods**. Biologists believe that a nursery group guarded by a protective parent provides security for the hatchlings. Some species of reptiles, such as the American alligator, stay in family groups for several years. Female American alligators have been observed at nest sites with newly hatched young as well as young from the previous few years. For other species of reptiles, the hatchlings stay together for only a few days, weeks, or months before striking out on their own. Hatchlings usually leave if an adult is not around, although some will form a pod even without an adult. The length of time a group of hatchlings stays together varies, depending on where they live.

American alligator hatchlings will often stay with their mother for several years.

Some crocodiles will gather in large groups to lie in the hot sun.

Adult Groups

Older crocodilians do not socialise with one another as much as they do when they are hatchlings. Adults form into groups only at certain times, such as when there is an abundant food source. Many species, such as American alligators and Nile crocodiles, may also bask in the warmth of the sun near other crocodilians.

When adult and juvenile crocodilians get together, the social group is organised by rank. Large, aggressive male crocodilians dominate the females, the juveniles, and the smaller, weaker males. These dominant crocodilians may even prevent others from getting access to mates, food, basking sites, and living space.

During the dry season or in times of drought, however, crocodilians seem to forget about rank. Large groups of all ages will gather around a water source. At these times, the reptiles appear to ignore one another as much as possible. They live together until the dry season is over. Fighting during this time is rare, even in cases where the crocodilians are extremely overcrowded. During a dry spell in Venezuela, about 200 common caymans lived without fighting at a water hole that was only 50 metres across and 2 metres deep. Although domination fights are rare during a drought, crocodilians may eat one another if the dry period is long and food remains scarce.

Communication

Crocodilians have developed ways to communicate with one another, both underwater and on land. They communicate by body language and by sound.

Before Birth

Crocodilians are able to communicate even before they hatch. Scientists have studied crocodilian eggs during their last two weeks of incubation. The results show that when an egg is tapped lightly, the unhatched crocodilian will answer by making a tapping sound. In one study, biologists buried a microphone in a nest. From this they discovered that unhatched crocodilians "talk" to one another by pecking against their shells. Baby crocodilians usually hatch on the same night. Biologists think the young reptiles may communicate in the eggs to make sure all the hatchlings emerge from their shells at once.

Crocodilian hatchlings make tapping noises as they hatch. These sounds may alert their mother, who sometimes helps them by carefully cracking their eggshells.

Body Language

The way a crocodilian holds its body tells a lot about the reptile's status. A dominant crocodilian shows its rank to another crocodilian by lifting its head, back, and tail out of the water. In the presence of a dominant crocodilian, a lower-ranked crocodilian sinks beneath the water, leaving only its head exposed. It then lifts its head up and opens its jaws. This means that it does not want to fight the higher-ranked reptile. If a low-ranked crocodilian does not do this, it is likely to be attacked and bitten by the higher-ranked reptile.

Sound

Crocodilians can make many different sounds, ranging from soft, hissing noises to loud bellows. These bellows can be heard easily from 150 metres away. They can be as loud as the engine of a small propeller aeroplane. A crocodilian bellows for 1 or 2 seconds, pauses, then repeats the call. Bellowing is often a group activity. When one crocodilian starts to bellow, others will join in. During the mating season, these bellowing choruses can last over half an hour. Alligators and caymans vocalise more than crocodiles and gharials.

Crocodilians also communicate with sounds they make with their bodies. They blow bubbles through the water and make purring sounds by breathing out through their nostrils. A crocodilian can also create vibrations in the water by rapidly squeezing its body muscles just beneath the water's surface. Other crocodilians can hear the sounds made by these vibrations. Many species use this form of communication during the mating season.

One of the most important sounds that a crocodilian makes is the headslap. The headslap is done at the surface of the water. The crocodilian first lifts its head out of the water. Sometimes it may stay in this position for a few minutes. Then it quickly opens and closes its jaws as if it is biting the water. This creates a loud pop and splashing noise that sounds like a flat shovel being slapped on the water. Some species, such as the American crocodile, will perform several headslaps in a row. A headslap is often answered with head-slaps from neighbouring crocodilians.

Crocodilians such as these Nile crocodiles can communicate on land and in water.

Hatchlings

It is up to the female crocodilian to build a nest, lay her eggs, and care for the hatchlings.

Opposite: Unlike most reptiles, female crocodilians are protective of their young. This alligator is guarding its nest from danger.

Crocodilians living in the tropics usually mate at the start of the rainy season. Crocodilians living in cooler regions usually mate in the late spring. Some species set up special mating territories. Others court and mate within their usual territory. The females of some species, such as the mugger crocodile, may mate twice a year. Most female crocodilians mate only once a year.

Male crocodilians try to mate with as many females as possible. Breeding groups of Nile crocodiles may have only one male to twenty females. In other species, a breeding group consists of one male and one female. Once mating has occurred, the males usually leave the females. It is up to the female crocodilian to build a nest, lay her eggs, and care for the hatchlings.

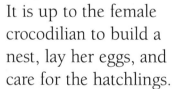

Sometimes hatchlings will bask in the sun or hitch a ride on their mother's back.

The Nest

All crocodilians build nests, and they are all very choosy about their nest sites. For eggs to hatch safely, a nest must be in an area that will not flood. Flooding is the major cause of breeding failure for many species of crocodilians. The temperature of the nest is also important for the survival of the **embryos**. For example, if temperatures in an alligator's nest fall below 27°C or rise above 34°C, the embryos may die.

Alligators, caymans, and some crocodiles build nest mounds out of plants and mud. As the plants decay in the sun, they give off heat, which helps to incubate the eggs. The smooth-fronted cayman nests in cool, shady rainforests. These caymans often build their nests beside termite mounds. Heat caused by the activity of the termites helps keep the eggs warm. Other crocodiles and gharials build nests by digging a hole in the sand with their hind feet. A female may use the same nest site for several years.

Crocodilians build their nests at night. Each nest can take a few days or even several weeks to finish. The nests vary in size depending on the species. An American alligator nest can be about two metres across and one metre high. The eggs are usually buried about 20 to 30 centimetres below the surface.

Crocodilians must be careful to build their nests in places safe from flooding. An unhatched crocodilian will drown if too much water seeps into its shell.

The Eggs

Crocodilian eggs have a tough, hard shell. This hard shell helps protect the embryo from insects, fungus, and germs. It can also protect the embryo from short-term flooding or drought.

Crocodilians lay their eggs at night. When a female crocodilian is ready to lay her eggs, she positions herself over the nest. One egg is laid about every 30 seconds. A crocodilian egg can be up to 10 centimetres long. A nest of eggs is called a **clutch**. Depending on the species, a clutch may contain 15 to 80 eggs. Usually larger, older females will lay more eggs than smaller, younger females.

When crocodilian eggs are laid, the young embryos are neither male nor female. Instead, they develop their sex as they incubate. During the first few weeks of incubation, temperature is very important. For crocodiles, eggs incubated at very warm or very cool temperatures will result in all female hatchlings. Temperatures in between will result in male hatchlings. For alligators and caymans, high temperatures mean all males, while low temperatures mean all females. Temperatures in between result in a mixture of female and male hatchlings.

Crocodilians incubate their eggs for about 2 to 3 months. In warmer regions, the incubation time is shorter than in cooler areas.

Although some crocodilian species will lay up to 80 eggs at a time, only a few eggs will hatch, and even fewer hatchlings will survive to adulthood.

Dangers in the Nest

Crocodilian hatchlings have a slim chance of surviving to adulthood. Up to 90 per cent of crocodilians die before even hatching.

Predators and flooding are the worst dangers to a nest of eggs. Predators include mammals, birds, other reptiles, and even insects. Ants can burrow under the sand and destroy a clutch of eggs. Larger animals dig up nests and eat the eggs. In Asia and Africa, monitor lizards eat more than half of all crocodilian eggs. In North America, raccoons, skunks, and black bears are common predators of crocodilian eggs.

Flooding also poses a danger because crocodilian eggs are **porous**, which means they are covered with tiny holes. These holes allow air to enter the egg so that a hatchling can breathe. However, during floods and heavy rains, the pores also allow water into the eggs. Floodwaters can drown a developing hatchling. Even if the hatchling does not drown, the damp egg might develop a fungus that will kill the hatchling. Bad eggs may then give off toxic gases that kill the hatchlings in other eggs. During a drought, the moisture inside an egg can evaporate through the pores. When this happens, the egg may dry out, killing the hatchling.

Albino crocodilians such as this American alligator rarely survive in the wild. Most crocodilians are well camouflaged.

Some hatchlings remain in the protection of a pod for several years.

Care

Crocodilians are very protective parents. As the young begin to break their shells, they make croaking noises. This lets the mother crocodilian know that it is time to dig open her nest. She carefully scrapes away the soil to expose the newly hatched young as well as any unhatched eggs. The mother then scoops up both hatchlings and unhatched eggs into her mouth. She can carry up to 20 eggs and hatchlings at once. She carries them to a nearby pool or other water source. Then she dips her head in the water and washes the hatchlings out of her mouth. Hatchlings are safer in the water, where they can dive beneath the surface if danger is present.

For her unhatched eggs, the mother rolls them carefully between her tongue and the roof of her mouth. This helps to crack the shells. With some species, such as the mugger crocodile, males may also carry hatchlings to the water.

Crocodilians are quick to protect hatchlings from danger. If a hatchling lets out a distress call, a parent or another adult will rush to its defence.

Development

Hatchlings

By the time a crocodilian is ready to hatch, it is already much longer than its egg. For example, an American alligator egg is only about 6 centimetres long. When it hatches, the hatchling inside is about 22 centimetres long. The small crocodilian fits by curling itself tightly inside the egg. An **egg tooth**, a hard, horny spot on the tip of a crocodilian's snout, helps the tiny reptile break free from the egg.

At this point in their lives, hatchlings often look quite different from their parents. Young crocodilians tend to be lighter coloured than adults. Some, like American alligators, also have striped tails and bodies.

A hatchling's coloration offers good camouflage from predators.

Juveniles

As young crocodilians grow older, they begin to darken to the colour of adults. At about four years old, they stop using juvenile calls and start to hiss and grunt like adults. Young crocodilians grow very quickly. By the time they are one year old, they may have tripled in size. A crocodilian's growth rate differs from species to species. For example, a cayman in Brazil may grow about 20 centimetres during its first year, and then only another 40 centimetres over the next 4 years. An American alligator may grow about 13 centimetres in a year.

Mammals are usually ready to mate once they have reached a certain age. Crocodilians are ready to mate when they have reached a certain length. Both the length and the number of years it takes them to reach this length can vary. In the Florida Everglades, alligators take about 14 years to reach maturity at 1.5 metres. In Louisiana, alligators are ready to mate at about 10 years of age and 2 metres in length.

As crocodilians grow, their chance of survival increases. Full-grown crocodilians have very few predators.

Habitat

Crocodilians need two kinds of habitats because they live both on land and in water.

Opposite: Crocodilians contribute to their habitat by feeding and excreting in the water. This helps to recycle the nutrients that keep the marshland alive.

A habitat is the place where an animal lives and grows. Crocodilians need two kinds of habitats because they live both on land and in water.

Dry land provides crocodilians with a place to warm themselves in the sun or to find shelter from rough water. In the summer, a crocodilian may cool itself in a burrow under a riverbank. In the winter, the reptile can escape from the cold by retreating to a burrow or mudhole. Crocodilians also need land on which to build nests and lay their eggs.

Water is just as important to crocodilians. It provides food and protection from the weather. Water also supports a crocodilian's body, helping it swim easily. Most crocodilians live in freshwater, but a few, such as the saltwater crocodile, can survive in saltier waters. Crocodilians usually prefer slow-moving water. In rough waters, waves can wash over a submerged crocodilian's nostrils, making it difficult to breathe. When water gets too rough, a crocodilian may retreat to the shore.

Crocodilians need habitats with places to warm themselves in the sun.

Crocodilian Territories

Crocodilians are **territorial**, which means they set up and defend a territory or home range. Dominant males establish territories that may consist of an entire pond or just one section of a river. This area includes basking places, food sources, and good wintering sites, such as burrows or mudholes. A male will not allow other males to enter his territory. During the mating season, a male patrols his range constantly, bellowing and slapping his head against the water. Most males will not hesitate to attack intruders and are especially aggressive during the mating season. With some species, this territory may be defended all year. The size of a territory varies, depending on the season, the species, and the rank of the individual crocodilian.

A female establishes a home range that overlaps with a male's home range. A female's territory always includes a nesting site. Females of some species defend a large area around their nest. Others nest in a group where they will defend only their own nest. Most females are aggressive when defending their nests.

Crocodilian territorial behaviour is most intense during the breeding and nesting season.

Surviving the Winter

American and Chinese alligators live in areas that become very cold during the winter. Sometimes it snows in these areas, and ponds and rivers freeze. At first, biologists thought that alligators escaped the cold by retreating to underground dens. The truth turned out to be quite different.

As temperatures fall during a cold spell, an alligator seeks shallow waters where ice is forming on the surface. The reptile submerges itself in the water, leaving only its nostrils poking out near the shallowest water. Its body points out from shore into gradually deeper water. Its nostrils create a small breathing hole in the ice. The rest of the alligator's body lies in the deeper, warmer waters. Although these deeper waters are warmer than the winter air above, they are still cold. Studies have shown that an alligator's body temperature can fall as low as 0° to 4°C while lying in this position. In some cases, the alligator's snout may even become frozen solid in the ice. As long as the breathing hole stays open, the alligator can survive until the ice melts.

Food

An adult crocodilian can survive for two years without a meal.

Opposite: This Nile crocodile is eating a Grant's gazelle in Kenya.

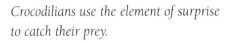

Compared to humans, crocodilians do not eat very much. Most eat only about fifty full meals a year. Crocodilians have a very efficient digestive system that is even capable of digesting bones. When a crocodilian eats, about 60 per cent of the energy from its food is stored as fat in its tail and on its back. By storing food as fat, a crocodilian can live a long time without eating. A hatchling can live up to 4 months without food. An adult can survive for 2 years without a meal.

Crocodilians eat only when the temperature is right – between 25° and 35°C. If temperatures dip below 25°C, the reptiles become sluggish and inactive. They need warmth to help them digest their food. If the weather remains cool, a crocodilian may simply regurgitate its meal. When temperatures rise above 35°C, crocodilians must concentrate on cooling themselves off rather than eating.

Crocodilians use the element of surprise to catch their prey.

What They Eat

Crocodilians will prey on just about any animal that comes their way. Prey can include insects, **amphibians**, birds, mammals, fish, or even other reptiles. The kind of prey a crocodilian eats depends on where the reptile lives and its size. Studies of the Nile crocodile show that hatchlings eat only small insects, frogs, and spiders. Young adults that are 2.4 to 3 metres long prey mostly on fish, although they also eat snails, reptiles, mammals, and birds. Larger adults prefer to eat larger mammals along with a few reptiles and fish.

Gharials and some crocodiles eat a lot of fish because their long, thin snouts are ideal for catching slippery prey. Alligators and other crocodiles use their strong, broad snouts to hunt large mammals, such as deer, hogs, and wildebeests.

In one meal, an adult crocodilian can eat 20 per cent of its body weight. It usually takes about 3 to 7 days to eat and digest such a large meal.

Crocodilians eat larger animals by tearing away big chunks of flesh. Some crocodilians even wedge their prey in between rocks or tree trunks. These act like vice grips, holding the animal in place so the crocodilian can rip it apart more easily. Once the crocodilian has a mouthful of food, it lifts its head high, using gravity to help the food go down.

A crocodilian will juggle its catch until the food can easily slide down its throat. This alligator is swallowing a turtle whole.

The Food Cycle

A food cycle shows how energy, or food, is passed from one living thing to another. Crocodilians survive by eating many different animals. These same creatures benefit from other things that crocodilians do during their daily lives. As you can see from this cycle, many plants and animals depend on crocodilians to survive. How many of these creatures would survive if crocodilians disappeared from the cycle?

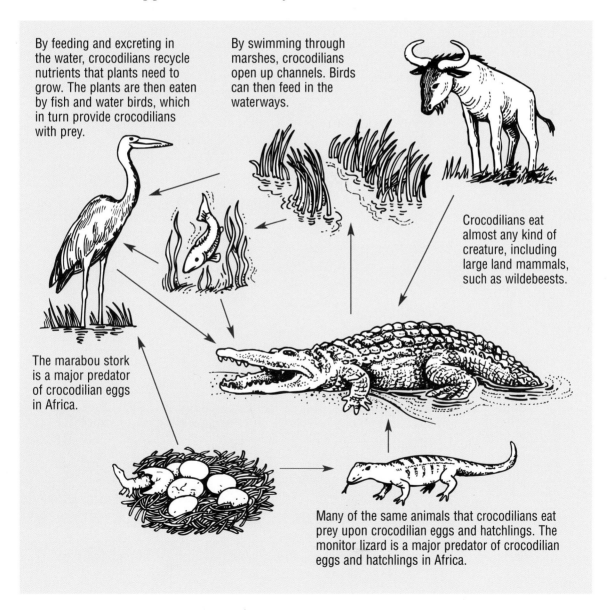

By feeding and excreting in the water, crocodilians recycle nutrients that plants need to grow. The plants are then eaten by fish and water birds, which in turn provide crocodilians with prey.

By swimming through marshes, crocodilians open up channels. Birds can then feed in the waterways.

Crocodilians eat almost any kind of creature, including large land mammals, such as wildebeests.

The marabou stork is a major predator of crocodilian eggs in Africa.

Many of the same animals that crocodilians eat prey upon crocodilian eggs and hatchlings. The monitor lizard is a major predator of crocodilian eggs and hatchlings in Africa.

37

How They Hunt

Crocodilians begin their hunt by lying motionless, waiting for prey to approach. When an animal gets close, the crocodilian snaps at it. Crocodilians can rush up onto a beach or jump almost vertically out of the water. Some larger crocodilians can leap 1.5 metres out of the water to snap at animals on the riverbank or low-flying birds over the water. Hatchlings catch dragonflies in the same way.

When hunting larger prey, a crocodilian aims for the sensitive nose or muzzle. The reptile lunges at an animal, grabs it by the muzzle, and pulls the animal towards the water. With its tender muzzle trapped between the crocodilian's sharp teeth, the prey animal usually walks to the water without trying to get away. Once its prey is in the water, the crocodilian drowns it by dragging it into deeper water. Sometimes a crocodilian grabs its prey and spins or rolls around and around in a "death roll". This helps to drown the prey and tear apart its flesh. Once the prey is dead, the reptile can feed at its leisure.

Crocodilians can hunt some animals that are more than twice their size, such as this wildebeest.

The ability to eat almost any animal has made crocodilians very successful predators. This American alligator is eating an immature little blue heron.

To hunt fish, a crocodilian lies in shallow water with its mouth open. Biologists think the reptile can sense the vibrations in the water when a fish swims near. The crocodilian snaps its jaws on the fish and then twists its head to pin the fish in the shallow water. If the fish is large, the reptile may even take it up onshore or hit it against the ground. Once the fish has stopped wiggling, the crocodilian positions the slippery meal in its mouth and gulps it down.

Crocodilians usually hunt alone. Most larger crocodilians hunt in areas where they have had previous hunting success. If there is an abundant food source, groups of crocodilians may hunt together. When schools of fish migrate, large numbers of crocodilians may work together to block off the school's passage. Once the fish are trapped, the crocodilians move in to feed.

Competition

Crocodilians that are over one metre long have almost no natural enemies or competitors.

Opposite: In highly populated southern Florida, alligators must often cross roads to get to their nesting grounds. Many are killed by accident.

Hatchlings are a target for many predators.

Young crocodilians are constantly in danger from predators. The smaller the crocodilian, the more likely it is to be eaten. Adult crocodilians rarely compete or enter into conflicts with other animals. Few creatures care to start a fight when faced with the sharp teeth and powerful jaws of a full-grown crocodilian. In fact, crocodilians that are over one metre long have almost no natural enemies or competitors. They compete only with their own kind and with humans. Competition with humans for territory can be dangerous for both the crocodilians and the humans.

Competing with Other Crocodilians

Some crocodilians begin competing with one another even before they become adults. For example, in Australia, officials banned crocodile-hunting after 30 years of overhunting. As a result, many more crocodiles survived. As the crocodile population grew larger, the juveniles began to eat the newly hatched young. Biologists think the young crocodiles were competing with one another for food.

While some researchers believe it is rare for crocodilians to eat one another, others think it is fairly common.

Adult male crocodilians compete with other males for mates and territory. These fights can be quite violent. In some cases, the conflict may even be fatal for the smaller, weaker male.

During times of drought, when crocodilians are forced to live in crowded conditions, some dominant males may try to keep others away from a food source. When food is plentiful, however, crocodilians often feed as a group. In Zambia, Africa, a group of 120 Nile crocodiles was observed eating a hippopotamus. The crocodiles swam around the carcass, each one waiting for its turn to eat. When an individual's turn came, it took a bite out of the prey and retreated to the edge of the group to eat it. Despite the large group, there was no fighting over the food.

Relationships with Other Animals

Although predators rarely attack adult crocodilians, it does sometimes happen. In Africa, Nile crocodiles may be killed by lions when the reptiles go up on land at night. In Central and South America, crocodilians may be preyed upon by jaguars or **anacondas**, large snakes that squeeze their prey to death. In southern Asia, leopards and tigers may kill both young and adult crocodilians.

In addition, large mammals, such as the hippopotamus, rhinoceros, and African elephant, may also kill crocodilians. This usually happens when the mammal is defending its young from a crocodilian attack.

The gharial's thin snout is better designed for eating fish than turtles. The turtle might not be so lucky near an alligator.

Conflicts with Humans

Of the 23 species of crocodilians, only a few will attack people. The American alligator, black cayman, mugger crocodile, orinoco crocodile, and American crocodile have all been known to attack and kill humans.

The two crocodiles that are most dangerous to humans are the Nile crocodile in Africa and the saltwater crocodile in southern Asia, the Pacific Islands, and Australia. Some attacks on humans occur when a crocodile is defending its territory or young. Others happen because some crocodiles see people as a food source.

Avoiding Attacks

Crocodilian attacks are often caused because people are not careful in areas where crocodilians live. If you are in crocodilian country, there are a number of things that you can do to prevent an attack. Test your knowledge with the quiz below.

1. You are in an area where crocodilians live. It is a hot day, and the river looks cool and inviting. You see a sign warning that there may be crocodilians in the area, but the paint on the sign is old and peeling. You will:

a) Put your bathing suit on and jump into the water. The sign is old so you think there are probably no longer any crocodilians around.

b) Stay out of the water and cool off with a cold drink.

c) Check the water carefully for crocodilians. If you do not see any, then you think it is OK to swim.

d) Take off your shoes and socks and cool off by wading along the edge of the water.

2. You are swimming in a river with a group of people. You are a strong swimmer and have managed to swim a short distance from the rest of the group. Suddenly, you see a crocodilian slip into the water close to you. You will:

a) Splash and yell to scare it away.

b) Swim quickly back to the group. The crocodilian will not attack a group of people.

c) Swim as quietly as possible to the shore and alert the other swimmers.

d) Stop swimming, stay calm, and keep quiet and still so the crocodilian does not notice you.

3. You are walking along a riverbank when you see a tiny crocodilian hatchling. You will:

a) Back away and leave the area.

b) Pick up the hatchling and help it into the water. You know that hatchlings are safest in the water.

c) Pick up the hatchling and take it home. It will make a great pet.

d) Look around for more hatchlings— maybe you will even find the nest.

4. You and your dog are out for a walk when you see a crocodilian basking in the sun with its back towards you. Luckily you happen to have your camera with you. It is the perfect chance for a great photo – if only the reptile was a little closer. You will:

a) Move closer to get the perfect shot. It will really impress your family and friends.

b) Throw small pebbles or sticks at the crocodilian so it will look over at you and you can get a better shot.

c) Send your dog over to distract the reptile so you can move closer.

d) Take out your telephoto lens and get a closer picture this way. Your family and friends will still be impressed.

Answers:

1. b) Always pay attention to warning signs, even if they look old and you do not see any crocodilians around. The reptiles may be hidden underwater where you cannot see them. If there is a sign up, do not swim or wade in the water. You should stay at least 3 metres from the water's edge. Remember, a crocodilian can lunge up onto the land to snatch you.

2. c) or d) The ideal thing to do is get out of the water quietly and quickly. If you cannot, try to stay as still and quiet as possible. By yelling and splashing, you will only alert the crocodilian to your presence, and it will come to see what the noise is all about. There is no safety in numbers. Crocodilians will not hesitate to attack a group of humans.

3. a) Leave the area right away. Wherever hatchlings are, an adult is probably close by. Do not try to pick up the hatchling. If you do, it will cry out a distress call. When this happens, any adult crocodilian that is in the area will come charging to the rescue.

4. d) Always stay at least 6 metres away from a wild crocodilian. Do not anger the reptile by throwing things at it. Crocodilians are good sprinters, and you may find yourself trying to outrun one. Try to keep pets away from crocodilians or any areas where the reptiles live. A dog or cat would make a tasty snack for a large crocodilian.

In the movie Crocodile Dundee, *actor Paul Hogan plays an Australian man who is famous for wrestling wild crocodiles.*

Folklore

Crocodilians appear in the folklore and myths of many cultures. These stories often reflect the way people feel about the reptiles. Most tales portray crocodilians as a menace. There are many stories about evil crocodilians that prey on helpless humans. In some cultures, however, crocodilians were once worshipped as gods or as sacred ancestors.

Crocodilians are a symbol of power in many cultures. As a result, crocodilian body parts were often used in medicines. It was thought that the reptile's power would help fight off sickness. In ancient Egypt, potions made from crocodile fat and dung were used to fight blindness. Romans believed that eating crocodile meat would cure children of whooping cough. In parts of Africa, crocodile fat or teeth were thought to protect people from being eaten by a crocodile. Some of these medicines were used for centuries. In the 1880s, Americans ate alligator oil and meat to fight off tuberculosis, a disease of the lungs. However, there is no proof that any of these medicines actually worked.

A sixteenth-century sea captain, John Hawkins, reported that crocodiles would attract prey by pretending to cry. When the prey animal approached to find out what was wrong, the crocodile would pounce. Crocodile tears are still a symbol of insincerity, even today.

Folklore History

In Egypt, the Nile River floods every year in September. This flooding brings nutrients to the soil, which is good for crops. The floods also bring a lot of crocodiles. Ancient Egyptians believed there was a link between good harvests and crocodiles. They worshipped crocodiles in the form of the god Sobek. Sobek was depicted with a human body and the head of a crocodile. In some parts of Egypt, crocodiles were dressed in gold costumes and were hand-fed by priests. When the reptiles died, their bodies were mummified.

Some African tribes believed crocodilians were sent by witches to carry out evil errands. In other parts of Africa and Southeast Asia, crocodilians were thought to be ancient relatives. People would tie their enemies to stakes along the river as a sacrifice to their crocodilian ancestors. In Madagascar, the spirits of tribal chiefs were said to live in the bodies of crocodiles. These crocodilian chiefs acted as judges. A person suspected of a crime was tossed into crocodile-infested waters. If the crocodiles ate the suspect, then the person was judged guilty of the crime.

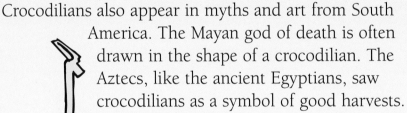

Crocodilians also appear in myths and art from South America. The Mayan god of death is often drawn in the shape of a crocodilian. The Aztecs, like the ancient Egyptians, saw crocodilians as a symbol of good harvests.

In Australia, crocodilians are important symbols in Aboriginal art and rock paintings. The oldest known picture of a crocodilian was found in Australia. Scientists believe the engraving is 30,000 years old.

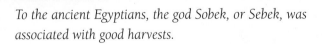

To the ancient Egyptians, the god Sobek, or Sebek, was associated with good harvests.

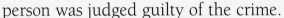

Crocodilians as Dragons

Dragons often appear in Chinese folklore and myths. They are seen as symbols of happiness, good harvests, and immortality. Where did the image of the dragon come from? Scholars think the earliest form of the dragon may have been a crocodilian.

Early Chinese descriptions of a dragon describe a creature with horns like a deer, a head like a camel, and a neck like a snake. It also had a belly like a crocodile, and claws like an eagle. This description does not sound much like a crocodilian. However, when scholars looked at ancient texts, they found the descriptions were quite different. These texts describe the dragon as a horned reptile with sharp teeth, claws, and a scaly body. Scholars now believe crocodilians were once important symbols in ancient Chinese cultures. Over time, the crocodilian symbol evolved into the image of a dragon. As people from different regions came together, they added other features to the image.

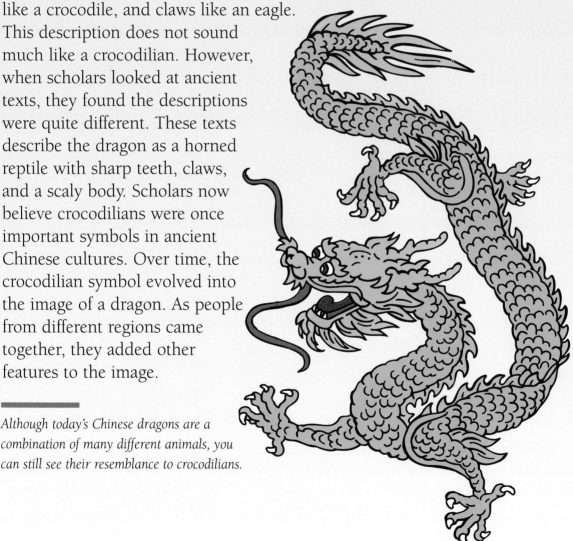

Although today's Chinese dragons are a combination of many different animals, you can still see their resemblance to crocodilians.

Folktales

Many different cultures have folktales about crocodilians. The folktale crocodilian may be a sly predator, or it may be tricked by other animals. In a few cases, the folktale crocodilian may even be kind and helpful. Here are a few tales you might enjoy:

How and Why Stories

In **African Wonder Tales**, a wife is forced to cook over a hot fire. The heat from the fire causes her to melt, and she runs into the river, where she becomes an alligator.

Carpenter, Frances. *African Wonder Tales*. New York: Doubleday, 1963.

The Cajun folktale **Why Alligator Hates Dog** explains how the feud between Alligator and Dog began.

Reneaux, J.J. *Why Alligator Hates Dog*. Little Rock: August House, 1995.

Discover why the alligator has a rough back in this collection of African-American folktales.

Faulkner, William. *The Days When the Animals Talked: Black American Folktales and How They Came to Be*. Chicago: Follett, 1977.

Evil Crocodilians

In **The Enormous Crocodile,** a crocodile lurks in hidden places, thinking up clever tricks for catching children. The other jungle animals try to foil his attempts.

Dahl, Roald. *The Enormous Crocodile*. London, Cape, 1978.

In one title in this collection, a kind cart driver carries a stranded crocodile back to the river. The ungrateful crocodile rewards the man's kindness by attacking his bull.

Brockett, Eleanor. *Burmese and Thai Fairy Tales*. Chicago: Follett, 1967.

In the third Akimbo story he is forced to brave crocodile-infested waters to save his friend, the crocodile man.

McCall Smith, A. *Akimbo and the Crocodile Man*. Methuen, 1995.

Foolish Crocodilians

In one story in this collection, a crocodile is tricked out of his intended prey by a clever jackal. In another story, a crocodile lying in ambush is tricked into blowing bubbles and giving away its hiding place.

Haviland, Virginia. *Favourite Fairy Tales Told in India*. William Morrow, 1995.

In *Safiri the Singer*, Hen tells Crocodile that he cannot eat her because they are brother and sister—after all, both came from eggs!

Heady, Eleanor. *Safiri the Singer*. Chicago: Follett, 1973.

Kind Crocodilians

In *Tales for the Third Ear from Equatorial Africa*, a young man shares kola nuts with a crocodile. In return, the crocodile helps the man find a ring in the river. With the ring, the young man can wed the chief's daughter.

Aardema, Verna. *Tales for the Third Ear from Equatorial Africa*. New York: Dutton, 1969.

In a Kenyan folktale in *Tales Told Near a Crocodile*, a man has the magical ability to call crocodiles. When he elopes with a rich man's daughter, he must use his magic to call the crocodiles to help him escape pursuit.

Harman, Humphrey. *Tales Told Near a Crocodile*. New York: Viking, 1967.

Endangered Crocodilians of North and South America

NORTH
AMERICA

30° N

ATLANTIC OCEAN

Equator

SOUTH
AMERICA

30° S

PACIFIC OCEAN

Critically Endangered
Orinoco crocodile
Cuban crocodile
Endangered
Black cayman
Vulnerable
American crocodile
Status Unknown
Morelet's crocodile

Status

There are now 17 crocodilian species that are endangered in all or some of the areas in which they live.

Many people believe that all crocodilians hunt humans. This has led to the persecution of all species, including those that do not eat people. Out of fear, people have destroyed nests and hunted adult and juvenile crocodilians.

Many crocodilian species are now protected from hunting. Unfortunately, many now face another danger – habitat loss. When forests are cut down for farms, rivers dry up or become silty. Pollution from cities and towns poisons waterways. Dams and canals flood nest sites and destroy habitat. All this means less living space for crocodilians. There are now 17 crocodilian species that are endangered in all or some of the areas in which they live.

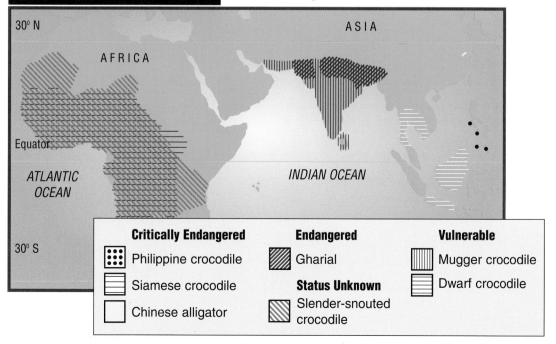

Endangered Crocodilians of Africa and Asia

The Skin Trade

People have always hunted crocodilians for food, medicine, or religious reasons. This kind of hunting did not cause crocodilian populations to decline seriously. Then, in the 1800s, people discovered that the skin from a crocodilian's belly made good, sturdy leather. People began hunting the reptiles for their skin, and crocodilian populations began to decline.

At first, only the large species were hunted for their skins. American alligators, Nile crocodiles, saltwater crocodiles, and New Guinea crocodiles were especially prized. The belly skin of these species has small scales and no bony osteoderms, making it perfect for tanning or making into leather. When these species began to disappear, hunters turned to other species, such as the black cayman and broad-snouted cayman. When these also began to disappear, hunters started killing the common cayman. The skins of these caymans were not ideal for tanning. Osteoderms made the belly scales unsuitable. As a result, hunters took only strips of skin from the throat and sides of the caymans. This meant that more caymans had to be killed to get the same amount of skin.

Between 1880 and 1933, about 2.5 million American alligators were killed in Florida. Another 3.5 million were killed during the same period in Louisiana. Similar numbers of crocodilians were killed in other countries. By the 1950s, 5 to 10 million skins were sold internationally each year.

Until people began killing crocodilians for their skin, hunting did not seriously harm crocodilian populations.

Wildlife Biologists Talk About Crocodilians

F. Wayne King

"A number of crocodilians remain perilously close to extinction...a real opportunity now exists for saving the remaining threatened species."

Wayne King is the Curator of Herpetology at the Florida Museum of Natural History. He is also Chairman of the World Conservation Union (IUCN) Crocodile Specialist Group, an organisation that is working to save endangered crocodilians.

Jeffrey W. Lang

"Crocodilians have a reputation for ferocity, but a closer look reveals that these unique reptiles exhibit many subtle and complex behaviours on a par with those of birds and mammals."

Jeffrey W. Lang has studied the behaviour of crocodilians living in Florida, Venezuela, Australia, Papua New Guinea, and India. He is Assistant Professor of Biology at the University of South Dakota in the U.S.A., as well as a Consulting Member of the IUCN Crocodile Specialist Group.

Frank J. Mazzotti

"Crocodilians are the most advanced of all reptiles...The success of [their] body design is evidenced by the relatively few changes that have occurred since crocodilians first appeared in the Late Triassic, about 200 million years ago."

Frank J. Mazzotti has been studying crocodilians in the United States and the Caribbean for over twenty years. He is a Wildlife Scientist in the Department of Wildlife, Ecology, and Conservation at the University of Florida in the U.S.A. He is also a member of the IUCN Crocodile Specialist Group.

Protecting Crocodilians

Before the 1960s, there were few laws to protect crocodilian populations. Hunting was uncontrolled. Most people saw crocodilians as dangerous predators. They believed that if someone could make money out of killing them, then all the better. Few people thought about saving the reptiles until populations began to decline seriously. As skins became harder to get, people started to realise that crocodilians were a valuable and endangered resource. By the late 1960s, countries that sold crocodilian skins began to bring in conservation laws.

In 1973 an international conference on endangered species was held in Washington, D.C. Eighty-one countries signed the Convention on International Trade of Endangered Species (CITES). This law banned the trade of parts or products from endangered species of plants and animals.

The law includes two separate lists. The first list is known as Appendix I. Endangered species are named here. According to the convention, trade of these species is against the law. The second list is Appendix II. It names all species whose populations are at risk but not yet endangered. Trade of these species is watched closely to make sure the populations do not become endangered.

All endangered crocodilians are listed on Appendix I. All other crocodilians are listed on Appendix II. Under the CITES law, all crocodilian species are protected in some way.

The biggest danger to crocodilians now is habitat loss due to human activity.

Viewpoints

Should saving crocodilians include keeping them on farms and ranches?

In the last few decades, many people have begun farming crocodilians. The reptiles are bred, raised, and killed for their skins. These are sold to make items such as boots, bags, and belts. Farms rely on captive breeding to get their stock. Ranches take eggs and hatchlings from the wild.

PRO  **CON**

1 In the past, crocodilians that posed a threat to humans or livestock were shot. Farms now provide a place for problem crocodilians to go. Some endangered species live on farms and are bred successfully.

2 Farm-raised crocodilians usually have better-quality skins than wild crocodilians. These skins can be processed and tanned at a cheaper price. This helps in the fight against poachers because illegal hunting is no longer as profitable.

3 Farming and ranching have changed people's views of crocodilians. Now the reptiles are seen as valuable resources rather than dangerous predators. This changed attitude has led to more studies and more protection for wild populations.

1 Farms are more concerned with producing skins than preserving species. Some crocodilians, such as the Siamese crocodile, are almost extinct in the wild. The last few live on farms in Thailand. However, these farms allow different species of crocodilians to interbreed. Soon purebred Siamese crocodiles may become extinct.

2 By selling any crocodilian skins, even those from a farm, people create a demand for them. Such a demand increases the risk that poachers will kill wild crocodilians.

3 We should not base conservation decisions on how valuable an animal may be to us. Crocodilians should be saved because they have the right to live in the wild, not because people can make money by trading their skins.

What You Can Do

By learning more about crocodilians, you can make better decisions about how to help them. Write to these organisations to get more information:

Conservation Groups

GREAT BRITAIN

British Herpetological Society
Zoological Society of London
Regent's Park
London NW1 4RY

eia Environmental Investigation Agency
69-85 Old Street
London EC1V 9HX
E-mail: eiauk@gn.apc.org
*The **eia** conducts in-depth research, and daring undercover investigations into illegal trade in endangered wildlife.*

Association for the Study of Reptiles
Cotswold Wildlife Park Ltd
Burford, Oxford
OX18 4JW

Fauna & Flora International
Great Eastern House
Tenison Road
Cambridge
Cambridgshire CB1 2DT
E-mail: info@fauna-flora.org

World Wide Fund for Nature (WWF-UK)
Panda House, Weyside Park
Godalming, Surrey
GU7 1XR

INTERNATIONAL

Endangered Wildlife Trust
The Goldfields
Environmental Centre
Johannesburg Zoological
Gardens
Private Bag X11
Parkview 2122
South Africa

World Conservation Union (IUCN)
28 rue Mauverney
CH-1196 Gland
Switzerland

Crocodilians on the Internet

You can learn about crocodilians by using the Internet. The Crocodile Specialist Group is an international network of people working to conserve the world's crocodilians. Visit their Web page to find out the latest information about crocodilians. You can read about recent surveys as well as the latest conservation plans. You will also find a list of other interesting crocodilian sites on the World Wide Web. **http://www.flmnh.ufl.edu/natsci/herpetology/crocs.htm**
Also have look at the Websites for:
The Endangered Wildlife Trust: http://ewt.org.za
Natural History Museum Book Services: http://www.nhbs.com

Twenty Fascinating Facts

1 The word "alligator" comes from the Spanish word *el largarto*, which means "lizard".

2 A crocodilian has no lips, so its mouth leaks even when it is closed. To keep from drowning when underwater, a crocodilian has a large flap of flesh at the back of its mouth. This flap keeps water from going into the reptile's lungs while it is underwater.

3 Crocodilians have a reflective layer in their eyes. At night, whenever bright light shines on the reptiles, their eyes appear to glow. Wildlife biologists can shine flashlights into swamps and count the pairs of glowing eyes to determine how many crocodilians may be in the area. Hunters may also find crocodilians with this method. This kind of hunting is illegal in some states in the United States. It is legal in other states only during the hunting season.

4 Alligators are the noisiest members of the crocodilian order. During the mating season in late spring, their bellowing can be heard throughout the marshes and swamps where they live.

5 Crocodilians are amphibious. This means that they live both in water and on land.

6 A crocodilian can never bite its tongue because it is attached to the bottom of its mouth.

9 The smooth-fronted cayman builds its nest beside termite mounds. Sometimes, while the eggs are incubating, the termites extend their mound right over the eggs. Young hatchlings cannot break through the hard termite cement and must rely on their parents to help dig them out.

10 Some female crocodilians use the same nests each year. Sometimes a female may even use the nest of another female. When this happens, two clutches may be laid in the same nest.

11 Parental care often begins even before the young hatch. Some female crocodilians stand guard over their nests. A female may even go without food until her eggs have hatched to protect her nest from predators. If it rains, she may stand right over the nest to shield it from the storm.

12 The young of many species have different markings to those of their parents. These markings may even differ within a species, depending on the incubation temperature of the eggs. Studies have shown that alligator hatchlings incubated at 33°C have one more stripe than hatchlings that have been incubated at 30°C.

13 Australians call saltwater crocodiles "salties" because the reptiles can live in saltwater as well as freshwater.

14 Crocodilians have a two-part stomach. The first part is called a gizzard. The gizzard contains many small pebbles that the crocodilian has swallowed. Some biologists believe these stones help the gizzard's muscles grind food. In the second part of the stomach, acids digest the ground-up food.

7 During the mating season, male crocodilians are very aggressive. In many cases, a female must show submissive behaviour in order to get the male to mate with her. As the two begin courting, they bump snouts, rub against each other, and blow bubbles underwater.

8 Nest flooding is the major cause of breeding failure for many crocodilian species. American alligator eggs can survive a flood for up to 12 hours. After this, the embryos begin to die.

15 When hunting, crocodilians rely on camouflage. They lie very quietly underwater, often among a bunch of reeds or just beneath a fallen tree. This makes them almost impossible to see.

16 When food is plentiful, crocodilians can grow faster – up to half a metre per year. If food is hard to find, their growth rate is much slower.

17 Building a house in areas where crocodilians live can be dangerous for both humans and reptiles. In some places, crocodilians crawl onto roads at night and are killed by passing vehicles.

18 In Ancient Egypt, crocodiles were considered to be gods. The centre of crocodile worship was a city known to the Greeks as *Crocodilopolis*.

19 In recent years, many species of crocodilians have begun to compete with humans for territory. In Florida, between 1948 and 1971, there were fewer than ten unprovoked attacks by alligators. Nobody was killed. In the early 1970s, Florida's human population grew rapidly. Towns and neighbourhoods expanded into alligator habitat. From 1973 to 1988, there were 90 attacks by alligators. Five people were killed.

20 The CITES law on the trade of endangered species has helped crocodilian populations recover from overhunting. Now conservation measures must focus on preserving crocodilian habitat. Loss of habitat is the greatest danger crocodilians face today.

Glossary

amphibians: Animals that live both on land and in water.

anacondas: South American snakes that can grow up to 9 metres in length. Anacondas squeeze their prey to death.

clutch: A nest of eggs.

crocodilians: The order of reptiles that includes alligators, crocodiles, caymans, and gharials.

egg tooth: A temporary horny growth on the tip of a hatchling's snout.

embryos: The unborn young of an animal.

hatchlings: Newly hatched animals.

keratin: A hard, hornlike material that forms the scales on the body of a crocodilian.

nocturnal: A word used to describe any animal that is most active at night.

osteoderms: Small bony plates located on the inner layer of crocodilian skin.

pods: A group of hatchling crocodilians.

porous: Containing many tiny holes, or pores.

quadruped: A creature that walks on four legs.

scales: Thin, flat plates that make up a crocodilian's outer layer of skin.

scutes: Large scales or plates that stick up or out to the side from the rest of a crocodilian's skin.

territorial: A word used to describe animals that set up and defend territories.

thecodonts: A group of extinct animals from which crocodilians, birds, and dinosaurs evolved.

Suggested Reading

Alderton, David. *Crocodiles and Alligators of the World*. Blandford, 1993.

Behler, John and Deborah. *Alligators and Crocodiles*. Colin Baxter Photography, 1998.

Bright, Michael. *Alligators and Crocodiles*. Franklin Watts, 1990.*

Deeble, Mark and Stone, Victoria. *The Crocodile Family Book*. North South, 1994.

Dow, Lesley. *Alligators and Crocodiles*. New York: Facts on File, 1990.

Nicol, J. *The Ganges Gharial*. Channel Four Television, 1984.

Pooley, A.C. *Discoveries of a Crocodile Man*. Johannesburg: Collins, 1982.

Ross, Charles, ed. *Crocodiles and Alligators*. Merehurst, 1989.

Stoops, Eric D; Stone, Debbie Lynne. *Alligators and Crocodiles*. Sterling Juvenile Books.*

Taylor, Dave. *The Alligator and the Everglades*. Crabtree, 1990.

* denotes a children's book

Index